LOVE IN FOCUS

1

Yoko Nogiri

CONTENTS

When I was little, my grandfather and I were joined at the hip.

He was a photographer, and he taught me how to take pictures.

Ever since then...

...my camera has been my life.

FILM 1

Hello, Springtime
of Life

LOVE IN FOCUS

IT HAS A COLLAR.

IS IT A RUNAWAY?

HEFF HEFF

PUPPY!

SNAP
カシャ

SNAP
カシャ

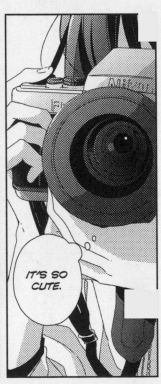

IT'S SO CUTE.

Oops.

...

?

I'M SO SORRY!

ガラ RATTLE
ガラ RATTLE
ガラ RATTLE

Runs away.

Aahh, that was scary.

BOFF ボ

!

Well, it was my fault.

は
あ.
WHEW

HE DIDN'T HAVE TO GET SO MAD, JUST 'CAUSE HE ENDED UP IN A PHOTO.

He looked kinda dorky, too.

Ah, ha ha.

WHAT A BIG RESPONSIBILITY!

AND MOM SAID SHE'S NOT WORRIED ABOUT ANYTHING AS LONG AS I'M WITH YOU, KEI-CHAN.

I BULLDOZED HIM INTO IT BY SAYING NO OTHER SCHOOL HAS A PHOTOGRAPHY CLUB WITH A PROFESSIONAL PHOTOGRAPHER FOR AN INSTRUCTOR.

Yeah.

BESIDES...

...IF GRANDPA WERE ALIVE...

...HE PROBABLY WOULD HAVE SUPPORTED MY CHOICE.

When I was in sixth grade, Grandpa got sick...

...and couldn't get out of bed anymore.

YOU MAKE IT SOUND SO NOBLE.

Noo!

THAT YOU STARTED TAKING PICTURES, AFTER ALL.

IT *WAS* FOR OLD MAN SAKAE

"I want you to go out there and see all that I can't."

To honor that request...

"And if you take pictures, please show them to me."

And right when it started getting really fun to take photos...

It just made me so happy to see him happy.

I started taking a camera everywhere I went.

...Grandpa passed away.

I'd lost my purpose and was just drifting...

There's a great teacher at my photography club.

...when my longtime friend, Kei-chan, who's a year above me, invited me to his school and I jumped at the chance.

BUT YOU HAVE TO BE CAREFUL.

And I came to live in this town, a three-and-a-half-hour-train ride from home.

Sigh.

YOU'RE ABOUT TO START A COMMUNAL LIFE WITH STRANGERS AT THE BOARDING HOUSE. YOU NEED TO PULL YOURSELF TOGETHER.

Just like how you got lost today.

YOU'VE ALWAYS HAD A HABIT OF LOSING SIGHT OF EVERYTHING ELSE WHEN YOU GET ABSORBED IN YOUR PHOTOGRAPHY.

DAD SAID THE EXACT SAME THING.

WELL, I CALL THEM STRANGERS...

...BUT PRETTY MUCH EVERYONE WHO LIVES HERE...

...IS A MEMBER OF OUR HIGH SCHOOL'S PHOTOGRAPHY CLUB.

A triangle roof.

Put your shoes in there.

Okay.

SO I DON'T THINK YOU HAVE TOO MUCH TO WORRY ABOUT.

THEY'RE ALL FUN PEOPLE.

OH, GOOD, AKAHOSHI-KUN. YOU FOUND HER.

YAE-SAN.

I WAS SO WORRIED WHEN HE TOLD ME YOU WERE LOST.

YES, THANK YOU FOR HAVING ME!

Here's your room key.

IF YOU HAVE ANY TROUBLE AT ALL, JUST COME TO ME.

I'M YAE HASUMI, THE LANDLADY HERE AT HASUMI INN.

MAKO MOCHIZUKI-SAN, RIGHT? WE MET WHEN YOU CAME TO VIEW THE PROPERTY, BUT LET ME INTRODUCE MYSELF AGAIN.

18

THE FLOOR PLAN IS POSTED ON THIS BULLETIN BOARD.

THIS IS ALSO WHERE YOU CAN CHECK WHO'S ON CLEANING DUTY.

I'LL GIVE YOU THE QUICK TOUR.

YEAH, THANKS!

Well, I'm off to buy groceries for lunch.

Take care!

3 | Entryway | 2
Bath / Toilet

2 F
WC | Bath | 5
Dishes
Bath
Toilet
6 | 7 | 8 | 9

Across from me.

YOU'RE IN ROOM 9, MAKO.

THE FLOORS AREN'T DIVIDED FOR BOYS AND GIRLS?

NOPE. I THINK SHE CAN'T DO THAT BECAUSE THE RATIO OF BOYS TO GIRLS CHANGES EVERY YEAR.

BUT ALL THE ROOMS HAVE LOCKS.

WE DO HAVE SEPARATE BATHS.

Girls on the first floor, boys on the second.

I SEE.

THAT DOOR RIGHT THERE LEADS TO THE SINK AND BATH.

THE TOILET IS THE DOOR PAST THAT.

AT THE END OF THE HALL ARE THE DINING AND LIVING ROOM.

Everything else is somebody's room.

SO ARE YOU READY TO SEE THE SECOND FLOOR?

Yeah.

...IT SMELLS LIKE WOOD.

CREAK
ギシ。

It's a new life.

SNAP

I can do this.

...HEY.

IS THIS ALL YOUR STUFF? IT'S NOT A LOT.

WELL, THE ROOM ALREADY HAS A DESK AND SHELVES AND STUFF.

AND I FIGURE IF I NEED OTHER SEASONAL CLOTHES, I CAN HAVE MY PARENTS SEND THEM OVER.

AS LONG AS I HAVE MY CAMERA, THE REST WILL WORK ITSELF OUT.

Everything in the backpack is camera gear.

RATTLE

ARE YOU SAYING I HAVEN'T GROWN UP?

I meant it in a good way.

YOU HAVEN'T CHANGED AT ALL, HUH, MAKO.

ARE

Huh?

AMEMURA-KUUUN!

THIS IS MAKO MOCHIZUKI, MY GOOD FRIEND FROM BACK HOME.

SHE'S A NEW FIRST-YEAR JUST LIKE YOU, SO BE NICE, OKAY?!

...

HMPH

...I DO SEE THAT, YES.

SO...AS YOU CAN SEE, HE LIKES TO PLAY IT COOL.

My new life...

...is getting off...

You got it!

IT'S ALMOST TIME FOR LUNCH.

SO COME ON DOWNSTAIRS AFTER YOU GET SOME UNPACKING DONE, OKAY?

The dining room will be down the hall to your right.

YOU CAN USE THE DISHES IN THAT CUP-BOARD.

I SEE.

YAE-SAN PREPARES MEALS FOR US.

AND WE ALL JUST SERVE OUR-SELVES.

OH, BY THE WAY, WHERE ARE *YOU* FROM, AMEMURA-KUN?

Is it just us three?

WHERE'S EVERYONE ELSE?

Labe your things with your name

THEY'RE ALL HOME FOR THE BREAK RIGHT NOW.

Oh.

...I WANTED... TO GO NORTH.

North?

...

TOKYO.

What?

SO WHAT BRINGS YOU ALL THE WAY UP HERE TO HOKKAIDO?

And even moving into a boarding house on top of that!

UH, YEAH. I INVITED MAKO.

You're not even the same age.

IT'S NOT VERY COMMON FOR CHILDHOOD FRIENDS TO MOVE AWAY FROM HOME TO GO TO SCHOOL TOGETHER.

WHAT ABOUT YOU?

WHEN WE WERE LITTLE,

MAKO'S GRANDPA TAUGHT US BOTH ABOUT PHOTO-GRAPHY.

AND WE GOT HOOKED ON CAMERAS.

AND ASAHI HIGH HAS A PROFESSIONAL PHOTOGRAPHER ALUMNUS WHO TEACHES AT OUR CLUB, SO...

Here we are.

He's mad...

...at me...

...isn't he?

...

...WHAT
ARE YOU
DOING?

Omochi ♂, age 6 the landlady's dog.

A celebrity who has the run of the house.

OH, WELL, IT'S OMOCHI.

SO I WANTED TO GET A PICTURE FROM A DOG'S EYE VIEW.

HE JUST LOOKED SO PERFECT, LYING THERE LIKE THAT.

AND THAT'S A REASON TO BE SPRAWLED ACROSS THE HALLWAY?

Eh heh.

MY GRANDPA ALWAYS SAID...

"WHEN YOU WANT TO TAKE A PICTURE, IT'S BECAUSE SOMETHING MOVED YOUR HEART."

"SO ALWAYS CHERISH THAT FEELING."

"DON'T LET IT GET AWAY,"

YUP.

Oh.

MY GRANDPA WAS A PROFESSIONAL PHOTOGRAPHER.

HIS NAME IS SAKAE MOCHIZUKI. HE'S PUBLISHED SOME PHOTO COLLECTIONS.

I did it again...

Just when I thought things were getting better...

MAKO-CHAN!

THEY'RE COMING TO FIX IT TOMORROW, SO COULD YOU ASK THE BOYS TO LET YOU USE THE ONE UPSTAIRS TODAY?

I'M SO SORRY. I CAN'T SEEM TO GET THE WATER HEATER WORKING FOR THE FIRST FLOOR BATH.

NO PROB-LEM!

YES?

KNOCK KNOCK

COME IN!

HEY, KEI-CHAN.

THE FIRST FLOOR WATER HEATER IS BROKEN, SO I'M SUPPOSED TO USE THE SECOND FLOOR BATH TONIGHT.

OH, OKAY.

THEN YOU CAN GO IN FIRST!

I WANT TO GET TO A GOOD STOPPING POINT BEFORE I PUT THIS BOOK DOWN.

OKAY.

WELL, DON'T MIND IF I DO!

Sure thing.

Bath...

Bath time~

Bath time~

KA-CHAK

WILL YOU LET ME TAKE YOUR PICTURE?

I want to capture Amemura-kun on film.

...DID YOU NOT HEAR A WORD I SAID?

I HATE PICTURES AND I HATE MY FACE.

HELL NO, YOU CAN'T TAKE MY PICTURE.

PORTRAITS DON'T ACTUALLY *HAVE* TO INCLUDE SOMEONE'S FACE.

AND YOU HAVE A NICE BODY, AMEMURA-KUN.

I COULD TAKE A PICTURE FROM BEHIND YOU.

OR JUST YOUR ARMS OR LEGS IF YOU WANT!

OKAY! THEN I'LL TAKE ONE WITHOUT YOUR FACE!

HUH?

WOULD THAT BE OKAY?

it's because something moved your heart.

When you want to take a picture,

My new
life has
begun...

...under
the triangle
roof.

LOVE IN FOCUS

FILM 2
Welcome to the
Photography Club

LOVE IN FOCUS

I wonder...

I...

...don't like my face.

And setting up a powerful barricade against me.

"Stay away from me" aura!

My brand new uniform.

Still kind of stiff.

...if there's some reason he would say that?

FWIP

COME IN!

KA-CHAK ガチ

MAKO, YOU READY?

KNOCK KNOCK

OH!

THAT'S NICE! THE UNIFORM LOOKS GOOD ON YOU.

KEI-CHAN IS TOO SWEET TO HIS CLOSE FRIENDS.

THANK YOU!

VERY CUTE.

SO YOUR MOM AND DAD SAID THEY COULDN'T MAKE IT TO THE ENTRANCE CEREMONY?

YEAH. THEY HAVE WORK TO DO.

Oh, well!

THAT'S TOO BAD.

...

I REMEMBER *SOMEONE* WHO SAID THE SAME THING ABOUT THE BOARDING HOUSE AND THEN GOT LOST ON THE WAY.

IT'S OKAY. I WENT THERE BEFORE, WHEN I TOOK THE ENTRANCE EXAM.

BUT YOU JUST GOT BACK FROM THE OPENING CEREMONY.

DO YOU KNOW WHERE THE SCHOOL IS? SHOULD I WALK YOU THERE?

But...

...I can't believe...

OH.

...we're in the same class, too.

AMEMURA-KUN.

NICE TO SEE YOU...

"...AT SCHOOL, TOO!"

KA-PLING

Barricade

Well.

That's okay.

I'M NANOKA.

I'M KURUMI.

ALL OF US WENT TO THE NEARBY MIDDLE SCHOOL.

OH, YOU'RE NEW!

"Don't talk to me." Okay, I get it.

My new life is only just getting started.

I'm gonna take it slow and steady.

WOW, SAPPORO?

OH, I CAME FROM SAPPORO.

I'M MAKO.

Nice to meet you!

I THINK THE RESULTS ARE IN ONE OF THE *FIL-CON* MAGAZINES AN OLD STUDENT LEFT HERE.

WHAT?!

NO, THAT'S—

UGH, KEI-CHAN!

WOW! I'D LIKE TO SEE HER WORK.

MAKO-CHAN IS GOING TO BE OUR RISING STAR THIS TERM, KANŌ-CHAN.

SHE WON, LIKE, THE GRAND PRIZE IN AN ORION CAMERA COMPANY CONTEST.

AHA! HERE IT IS!

Grand Prize

"Mirror of Spring"

Let me see.

Fil-Con Life

IT'S UPSIDE-DOWN.

Upside-down?

B—

BUT IT'S...

AND YOU TOOK THAT WHEN YOU WERE 10?

I'm impressed.

I LOVE THIS!

WHOA! THAT'S BEAUTIFUL!

Cherry blossoms!

Because you never do anything with your pictures. They'd go to waste.

And Kei-chan picked it, and submitted it, without asking me.

SO IN MY MIND

THE ACTUAL PICTURE SHOULD HAVE THE REFLECTION OF THE CHERRY TREE ON TOP.

You know?

I WAS SO IN AWE WITH HOW NICE THE REFLECTION LOOKED IN THE PUDDLE...

TREMBLE

TREMBLE

...THAT I TOOK THE PICTURE LIKE THIS.

OH, I SEE WHAT YOU MEAN.

OF COURSE, I STARTED OUT AS AN ARTIST WHO ONLY TOOK REFERENCE PHOTOS FOR MY DRAWINGS.

I WAS LUCKY THAT PEOPLE WANTED MY PHOTOS, TOO, AND NOW HERE I AM...

SO MAYBE I SHOULD SAY "WE'RE IN THIS TOGETHER."

I...

...like this teacher.

AREN'T YOU GLAD YOU CAME HERE?

OKAY, YOU CAN HAVE THIS MAGAZINE AS A SOUVE-NIR!

OKAY, NOW THAT THE INTRODUC-TIONS ARE OVER...

WELL, THE KID WHO LEFT IT HERE OBVIOUSLY DIDN'T NEED IT.

WHAT? ARE YOU SURE?

UH-HUH!

AND NEWBIES DON'T GET TO SEE IT UNTIL THE PRESENTATION!

WE HAVE TO PREPARE OUR CLUB INTRODUCTION FOR THE WELCOME ASSEMBLY.

...WILL ALL NEW STUDENTS PLEASE LEAVE?!

BOOT
ホイッ

I see.

...

WELL, I'M HERE.

MIGHT AS WELL TAKE A LOOK AROUND THE SCHOOL.

I'm telling you!

Hmmm?

Come on!

Hm?

We'll cut it for you!

Is that...

I need to get help...

...Like a teacher or something.

GLANCE GLANCE
キョロキョロ

Very obviously being picked on.

...Amemura-kun?

They saw me.

Urk!

HEY, WHATCHA TAKING PICTURES OF?

N-NOTHING.

JUST GETTING PHOTOGRAPHIC EVIDENCE.

OH.

YOU THOUGHT WE WERE BULLYING HIM, DIDN'T YOU?

I THINK YOU MIGHT HAVE THE WRONG IDEA HERE.

···

LIKE HEY, MAYBE YOU CAN'T SEE WHERE YOU'RE GOIN' 'CAUSE OF THOSE RIDICULOUSLY LONG BANGS.

BUT WE WEREN'T!

HE BUMPED INTO US, SO WE WERE JUST GIVING HIM SOME TIPS, AS HIS SENPAI.

OH! WERE YOU JUST...

THEY'RE NOT WRONG.

As thanks, we'll cut your bangs!

No thanks. It's against my policy.

...

Your policy, eh?

Well, if that's your policy...

Here I was trying to come to his rescue.

But he ended up coming to mine.

TMP

TMP TMP

TMP

...YOU CAN'T BACK DOWN OR GET SCARED.

GUYS LIKE THEM ARE JUST GOOFING OFF. THEY DON'T MEAN ANY HARM.

Of course, that makes them even harder to deal with.

IT'S BEST TO JUST HUMOR THEM.

"He used to be one of them" theory

YOU KNOW AN *AWFUL* LOT ABOUT "GUYS LIKE THEM"...

DON'T GET ANY FUNNY IDEAS.

LISTEN.

Well

JOKING ASIDE.

I'M GLAD NOTHING HAPPENED!

...

ANYWAY.

I APPRECIATE THE THOUGHT.

THANKS.

パ SHUT ァ—ン.

Does this
mean...

...that
maybe...

...we're
a little bit closer
now?

AND
THE DAY
HE LETS ME
TAKE HIS
PICTURE IS
CLOSER,
TOO!?

TFF トス

No,
don't rush.
Take it
slow and
steady.

You
started
in the
negative,
after
all.

ZUP ずる

THUD
THUD

Capture
the light.

Orion Camera Company

ORION

Is this...

...Amemura-kun?

FILM 3

The Secret
Amemura-kun

LOVE IN FOCUS

I just can't find the right opportunity.

Communal living is tricky...

AND HERE AT SCHOOL, AS USUAL,

HE ACTS LIKE HE DOESN'T WANT ME TO TALK TO HIM.

I DIDN'T KNOW THE NICKNAME WAS THAT FAMOUS.

IS IT LENS INN, BY ANY CHANCE?

But it looks like I couldn't have been more wrong.

I thought we were closer now.

YEAH, THAT'S THE ONE.

HEY, MAKO?

I KNEW IT! OKAY, OKAY. SO DO YOU KNOW...

YOU SAID YOU WERE STAYING AT A BOARDING HOUSE, RIGHT?

HM?

I WON'T BE GOING HOME FOR GOLDEN WEEK, EITHER.

I KNOW MOM WON'T LIKE IT.

TELL HER I'M SORRY FOR ME, ANIKI*.

KEI-CHAN.

*A familiar way of addressing one's older brother.

CLICK

MAKO.

...YOUR MOM WAS WORRIED ABOUT YOU.

SINCE YOU DIDN'T GO HOME FOR SPRING BREAK, EITHER.

SORRY, KEI-CHAN. I KIND OF OVERHEARD.

WELL, IT'S MY FAULT FOR TALKING OUT HERE IN THE HALLS.

UH...

YEAH.

MY DAD WAS REALLY AGAINST ME COMING HERE, BUT I DID.

SO IT'S NOT VERY EASY FOR ME TO FACE HIM.

OH YEAH, HE DOESN'T WANT YOU TO BE A PHOTOGRAPHER.

Kei-chan's father...

...was always strict, even when we were little.

OH...

MM-HMM. HE PUTS ACADEMIC TRACK RECORDS FIRST, AND IS OBSESSED WITH STANDARDIZED TEST SCORES.

BUT

YOU'RE WORKING REALLY HARD TO STAY ON THE HONOR ROLL.

He's a doctor, and very stern.

HE COULD GIVE YOU CREDIT FOR THAT.

THANKS FOR SAYING THAT. YOU'RE THE ONLY ONE ON MY SIDE!

YOU ARE NOW...

...AND YOU WERE THEN.

THIS WAY.

...YEAH.

LET'S GO WITH THAT.

HIDE AND SEEK?

TMP
た...

AND...

...YOU TOOK ME BY THE HAND AND HID ME.

THAT'S RIGHT.

AND IT'S WHEN YOU STARTED LEARNING PHOTOGRAPHY FROM GRANDPA WITH ME.

Oh!

THAT'S WHEN I STARTED RUNNING AWAY TO YOUR HOUSE ALL THE TIME.

NOW, NOW. DON'T SAY THAT. SOOTHE YOUR BROTHER'S PAIN.

YOU KNOW, KEI-CHAN.

WHAT THE—?

I MEAN ...

YOU *ARE* MY LITTLE SISTER, AREN'T YOU?

YOU'RE STARTING TO GET HEAVY.

And I'm in my personal space.

"So he probably thinks of me as a little sister."

WELL, YOU WERE TALKING IN THE LIVING ROOM.

OH, SO YOU HEARD THAT, HUH?

WELL, NOT THAT I MIND.

So I over-heard.

SILENTLY JUDGING THEM

......

Oh! Amemura-kun!

WHA—

WHERE DID YOU...

...get that?

PHOTO CLUB. THEY LET ME HAVE ONE OF THEIR OLD MAGAZINES.

I JUST HAPPENED TO FIND THIS.

PETRIFIED

...THIS GUY IS SO EASY TO READ.

Grk!

Self-destructed!

Based on that reaction.

SO THIS MODEL REALLY *IS* YOU?

...SO WHAT IF IT IS?

ARE YOU GOING TO BLACKMAIL ME?

A RELATIVE OF MINE RUNS A CHILDREN'S CLOTHING COMPANY.

THAT'S HOW IT STARTED.

EVER SINCE I WAS FIVE, UNTIL I TURNED 12 OR SO...

MODELING, CHILD ACTING— THAT KIND OF THING.

WHEN I WAS LITTLE, I DIDN'T THINK ABOUT IT. I JUST DID WHAT I WAS TOLD.

Smile, smile!

What's wrong, Mitsuru-kun? You look so tense.

THE MORE THEY SAID, "BE MORE INNOCENT."

BUT THE OLDER I GOT,

"GIVE ME A BIGGER SMILE."

I REALIZED I WASN'T CUT OUT FOR THAT STUFF.

THE STRESS STARTED GETTING TO ME.

LIKE BEING MORE INNOCENT...

IT'S TRUE, I REALLY CAN'T IMAGINE AMEMURA-KUN BEING LIKE THAT.

ONE DAY, I GOT IN FRONT OF THE CAMERA...

I can't do it any-more.

...AND IT MADE ME SO SICK, I PASSED OUT.

SO WHEN I STARTED MIDDLE SCHOOL, I TOOK IT AS MY CHANCE TO QUIT.

BUT...

...IN MY HOMETOWN, PEOPLE STILL KNEW MY NAME... MY FACE...

psst
ひそ

ひそ
psst

He was in some commercial, wasn't he?

Him?

I EVEN HAD A STALKER.

THEY SENT ME WEIRD LETTERS AND FOLLOWED ME AROUND.

A STALKER?!

AND IT WAS A GROWN WOMAN.

104

...

SO HE'S LIKE... RETIRED.

SO I CAME NORTH.

AND LIVE MY LIFE IN PEACE AND QUIET.

THAT'S WHY I DECIDED TO GO TO A HIGH SCHOOL WHERE NO ONE KNOWS WHO I AM,

...I KEPT HAVING ALL THESE TERRIBLE EXPERIENCES BECAUSE OF HOW I LOOKED.

So...

...what I was doing...

...was basically opening up...

...his old wounds...

...wasn't it?

...I'M SORRY.

SO...

HE DISSED ME. RIGHT TO MY FACE.

WEIRD

WHAM

Weird

I GET THAT YOU'RE WEIRD.

...ALL RIGHT.

HERE ARE MY TERMS.

BUT I'M STARTING TO WONDER WHAT I LOOK LIKE THROUGH YOUR EYES.

My...

...eyes?

BUT...

...I WON'T TIE MY HAIR BACK, AND I WON'T TAKE MY GLASSES OFF.

IF THAT'S OKAY, THEN YOU CAN DO IT.

Uh, yeah.

THAT'S TOTALLY FINE.

OKAY.

FILM 4

The First Photo
Shoot

WOW, THESE ARE PRETTY!

I CAN'T BELIEVE HOW VIVID THE STARS LOOK!

WHERE DID YOU TAKE THESE?

In the mountains?

I THINK THOSE ARE THE ONES I TOOK FROM MY SUMMER HOME.

LOVE IN FOCUS

THAT'S THE PLACE WE USED FOR OUR CLUB'S CAMP LAST YEAR, ISN'T IT?

His summer home?!

THAT'S RIGHT.

IF EVERYONE CAN MAKE IT, WE SHOULD DO IT AGAIN THIS YEAR.

I SEE. A PRINCE INDEED.

SO BOURGEOIS...

But then why would he be living at a boarding house?

Oh!

THIS IS THE ONE I TOOK FROM THE ATTIC RIGHT HERE AT THE BOARDING HOUSE.

Dish-washing duty for the day

WHAT?

HUH? DIDN'T I MENTION IT WHEN I GAVE YOU THE TOUR?

WE HAVE AN ATTIC? WHERE...?

HMM.

NO! NOT EVEN ONCE!

WC BATH 5

6

7 8

Oohh.

YOU SAW HOW THE ROOM ON THE LEFT END OF THE SECOND FLOOR DIDN'T HAVE A NUMBER, RIGHT?

YOU CAN GET TO THE ATTIC FROM THERE.

I THOUGHT THAT WAS SOMEBODY'S ROOM.

BUT USUALLY SAIONJI-SENPAI IS CAMPED OUT THERE.

LEAVING ALL HIS EQUIPMENT LYING AROUND.

IT'S A COMMON AREA, SO WE'RE ALL ALLOWED USE IT.

IT'S A LOT OF WORK LUGGING IT UP AND DOWN THE STAIRS EVERY TIME.

I'LL HAVE TO CHECK IT OUT LATER.

Wow.

I always wanted an attic view!

SO DO YOU ONLY TAKE PICTURES OF STARS, SAIONJI-SENPAI?

I PREFER FOR GIRLS TO CALL ME LUCAS ♡

AND BY THE WAY.

How is he... so sparkly...

OH, I DON'T LIMIT MYSELF. I PHOTOGRAPH ANYTHING I FIND BEAUTIFUL.

I AM A MAN WHO LOVES BEAUTY, AFTER ALL.

I SEE...

SQUEEZE

HE'S QUITE THE CHARACTER.

LUCAS-SENPAI DOES LOVE THE LADIES.

There he goes again.

Boarding houses...

...really do have all kinds of people.

Retirees, for example.

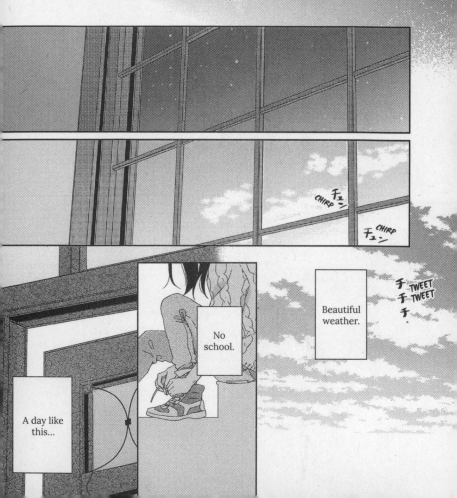

CHIRP チュン

CHIRP チュン

TWEET チ
TWEET チ
チ.

No school.

Beautiful weather.

A day like this...

I LOVE
THIS
AREA.

...or was he very emphatic just now?

Is it me...

ARE YOU TWO A COUPLE?

NO, NO, WE'RE JUST CHILDHOOD FRIENDS.

?

THAT'S THE SECOND TIME SOMEONE'S THOUGHT THAT...

I DON'T THINK "JUST" CHILDHOOD FRIENDS...

...WOULD HUG IN THE HALLS...

...OR DELIBERATELY MOVE FAR FROM HOME INTO THE SAME BOARDING HOUSE.

He was just playing around...

OH... THAT?

SO I'M GLAD I CAME HERE.

YOU...

Wait.

ARE YOU SAYING I'M STUPID?

...ARE APPALLINGLY GOOD AT LOOKING ON THE BRIGHT SIDE.

Eh heh.

IT'S MY ONLY GOOD TRAIT.

NO.

IT'S A COMPLIMENT.

カシャッ
SNAP

はぁ
SIGH

QUIT IT WITH THE SURPRISE ATTACKS.

You little...

Sorry.

OH YEAH, THE ATTIC.

I HAVEN'T GONE TO SEE IT YET.

CREAK キイ

Someone's up there?

...I START FEELING LIKE I SHOULD START LOOKING ON THE BRIGHT SIDE, TOO.

IT *IS* EARLY FOR YOU TO BE GOING INTO RETIREMENT!

ANYWAY, I COULD AT LEAST CUT MY HAIR.

IT *DOES* GET IN THE WAY.

...

I guess.

to be continued

WOW, LOOK AT THIS FEAST!

IT'S A WELCOME PARTY!

YOU CAN'T GUESS?

Someone's birthday?

ARE WE CELEBRATING SOMETHING?

FOR YOU AND AMEMURA-KUN.

WE FIGURED IT WAS A GOOD TIME, SINCE ALL THE TEN-ANTS ARE HERE, INCLUDING SAIONJI-SENPAI.

NENE AND I MADE DESSERT.

YAE-SAN PULLED OUT ALL THE STOPS COOKING THIS MEAL.

All you did was taste test, Nobu.

A welcome party!

TAKES THE SEAT OF HONOR LIKE HE OWNS IT

We're not doing it for you, senpai.

I'M SORRY YOU HAD TO DELAY IT.

ALL FOR ME.

WOW, WE'RE SO HONORED!

RIGHT, AMEMURA-KUN?

...THANKS.

OKAY, I'LL GO GET MY CAMERA.

To commemorate the event:

GOOD IDEA.

!

SINCE WE'RE ALL HERE, LET'S ALL TAKE A PICTURE TOGETHER!

RIGHT?!

WHEN WE'RE ALL TRYING TO HAVE FUN, YOU MUST ENJOY IT WITH US.

A COOPERATIVE SPIRIT IS VITAL TO COMMUNAL LIVING, AMEMURA-KUN.

Look who's talking.

I'll pass...

CLAMP ガシッ

Look who's talking Part 2 →

LUCAS-SENPAI IS SO PUSHY!

Go on. I'll even let you have the seat of honor.

Squeeze in, squeeze in.

I SET THE TIMER.

BEEP

BEEP

BEEP

BEEP

...I'M SO GLAD I CAME TO THIS BOARDING HOUSE.

NOW LET'S EAT BEFORE IT GETS COLD.

OKAY.

Good idea!

Let's post one on the bulletin board, too!

I'll print one for everyone later.

And I'm sure...

I'll feel that way for all three years that I'm here.

The end.

Afterword

Thank you very much for picking up this manga!

This tomato is a self-portrait.

Hello, or perhaps nice to meet you!

I'm Nogiri.

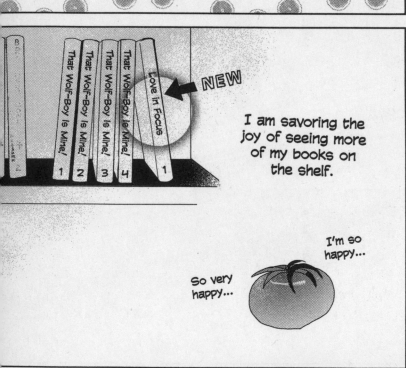

That Wolf-Boy is Mine! 1
That Wolf-Boy is Mine! 2
That Wolf-Boy is Mine! 3
That Wolf-Boy is Mine! 4
Love in Focus 1

NEW

I am savoring the joy of seeing more of my books on the shelf.

I'm so happy...

So very happy...

They never state it in the story, but the setting for *Love in Focus* is based on the town of Hakodate.

Before the series started, I got to go there with my editor for research!

So stylish!

Cobbled streets!

So... exotic!

So many cute cafés!

Tons of hills with names!

SNAP

SNAP

153

Special Thanks.

Aki Nishihiro-chan
A-H-chan
My friends and family.

Research Assistance:

Photographer
Hatsuki Hamamura-sama

Everyone from Hokkaido's
Hakodate Nishi High School.

My editor-sama.

Everyone in the Aria
editorial department.

Everyone who
was involved in the
production of this
book.

Everyone who read
this book...

Thank you very much!

I'll work hard on the next
volume, too!

Omochi ♂,
age 6

The
celebrity
of Lens Inn.

The
landlady's
pet dog!

...is really nice, and I love them.

C'mere, pup!

Omochi!

Everyone who lives here...

HMPH...

I don't love that.

Oohh, Omochi! You're squishy just like mochi!

...is kind of...

persistent.

The sparkly man...

OMOCHI.

But no matter what anyone says...

...Amemura-kun is my favorite!

Waaalk!

READY FOR YOUR WALK?

Triangle roof, page 17

The technical term for this type of roof is a "gable roof," referring to a roof made of two slanting sides with a triangular portion of wall, or "gable," between them. But Mako instead refers to the gable as the more familiar "triangle." The original Japanese title of the series is *Renzu-Sou no Sankaku*, or "The Triangle of Lens Inn."

WC, page 19

In Japan, the toilet is in a separate room from the bathtub. WC stands for "water closet," which is the polite term for such a room.

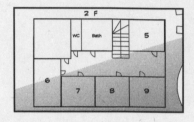

Entrance ceremony and opening ceremony, page 59

In Japan, at the start of a new school year (in April), schools will hold opening and entrance ceremonies for the students. The opening ceremony, more literally translated as "beginning of operations ceremony," is for returning students, and is where they find out whether or not they will be in the same class as the previous year. The entrance ceremony is for the students who are newly entering the school as first-years to introduce them to their new place of learning. These two ceremonies can be held in any order, and some schools have the opening ceremony first so that the returning students can sit with their new classes when they attend the entrance ceremony. Unlike the four-year system in the US, in Japan, there are only three years in high school.

TRANSLATION NOTES

Hasumi "Lens" Inn, page 67
While "Lens" is already an appropriate name for an inn housing most of a school's photography club, there's a reason that particular part of a camera is more appropriate than others. The name Hasumi is written with two Chinese characters that literally mean "lotus dwelling." In Japanese, Chinese characters usually have multiple pronunciations, and this particular pair can also be read as *ren-zu*, which is the Japanese pronunciation of the English word "lens."

Golden Week, page 93
Golden Week is the first week in May—a week so full of national holidays that everyone takes the whole week off. Naturally, this makes it a good time to travel.

Lucas Saionji, page 114
Being a quarter French, Saionji-senpai's given name is pronounced the French way, meaning the S is silent.

LOVE IN FOCUS

Hey, Mako. Looking at newly-developed photos?

The people in the background here are so fun, I can't stop looking at them.

Yea

Let me see!

...Tanuki cosplay?

Maybe they're tourists?

They're awfully excited.

Don't give it to me.

Got a cold, Aoshi?

Achoo!

Thank you for buying *Love in Focus* volume one!

Yoko Nogiri 野切 燿子

WAITING FOR SPRING

A sweet romantic story of a soft-spoken high school freshman and her quest to make friends. For fans of earnest, fun, and dramatic shojo like *Kimi ni Todoke* and *Say I Love You.*

KISS ME AT THE STROKE OF MIDNIGHT

An all-new Cinderella comedy perfect for fans of *My Little Monster* and *Say I Love You!*

LOVE AND LIES

Love is forbidden. When you turn 16, the government will assign you your marriage partner. This dystopian manga about teen love and defiance is a sexy, funny, and dramatic new hit! Anime now streaming on Anime Strike!

YOUR NEW FAVORITE ROMANCE MANGA IS WAITING FOR YOU!

THAT WOLF-BOY IS MINE!

A beast-boy comedy and drama perfect for fans of *Fruits Basket*!

"A tantalizing, understated slice-of-life romance with an interesting supernatural twist."
- Taykobon

WAKE UP, SLEEPING BEAUTY

This heartrending romantic manga is not the fairy tale you remember! This time, Prince Charming is a teenage housekeeper, and Sleeping Beauty's curse threatens to pull them both into deep trouble.

In love, there are no save points.

ヲタクに恋は難しい

WOTAKOI:
LOVE IS HARD FOR OTAKU

by FUJITA

Narumi has had it rough: Every boyfriend she's had dumped her once they found out she was an otaku, so she's gone to great lengths to hide it. At her new job, she bumps into Hirotaka, her childhood friend and fellow otaku. When Hirotaka almost gets her secret outed at work, she comes up with a plan to keep him quiet. But he comes up with a counter-proposal: Why doesn't she just date him instead?

Princess Jellyfish

Akiko Higashimur

**ALSO
AN ANIME!**

"One of the best
manga for beginners!"
—*Kotaku*

Tsukimi Kurashita is fascinated with jellyfish. She's loved them from a
young age and has carried that love with her to her new life in the
big city of Tokyo. There, she resides in Amamizukan, a safe-haven for
geek girls where no boys are allowed. One day, Tsukimi crosses paths
with a beautiful and fashionable woman, but there's much more to
this woman than her trendy clothes...!

A Kodansha Comics Trade Paperback Original
Love in Focus volume 1 copyright © 2017 Yoko Nogiri
English translation copyright © 2019 Yoko Nogiri

Published in the United States by Kodansha Comics, an imprint of
Kodansha USA Publishing, LLC, New York.

Publication rights for this English edition arranged through
Kodansha Ltd, Tokyo.

ISBN 978-1-63236-768-6

Printed in the United States of America.

www.kodanshacomics.com

9 8 7 6 5 4 3 2 1
Translation: Alethea and Athena Nibley
Lettering: Sara Linsley
Editing: Haruko Hashimoto
Kodansha Comics edition cover design by Phil Balsman